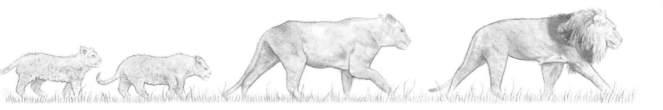

WHAT'S IT LIKE TO BE A

BABY LION?

Published in the United States in 1998 by
The Millbrook Press, Inc.
2 Old New Milford Road
Brookfield, Connecticut 06804

First published in Great Britain in 1998 by
Belitha Press Limited
London House, Great Eastern Wharf
Parkgate Road, London SW11 4NQ

Editor: Honor Head
Designers: Hayley Cove, Victoria Monks
Illustrator: Matthew Nicholas
Consultants: Sally Morgan, Wendy Body

Cataloging-in-Publication data is on file at the
Library of Congress

Printed in Belgium

Photo credits: BBC Natural History Unit: cover, pp. 22
(Anup Shah), 29 (top) (Gerry Ellis); Bruce Coleman
Ltd.: p. 27 (Gunter Ziesler); FLPA: pp. 11, 15, 19, 23
(Mark Newman), 21 (top) (Eichorn/Zingel), 21
(bottom), 26 (W. Wisniewski), 24 (top) (David
Hosking); Getty Images: pp. 13 (Renee Lynn), 14
(Mark Petersen), 29 (bottom) (Daniel J. Cox), 30 (Tim
Davis); Images of Africa: pp. 4, 18 (David Keith Jones);
NHPA: p. 24 (bottom) (Roger Tidman); Planet Earth
Pictures: pp. 6 (M & C Denis-Huot), 8, 10, 16-17, 17
(top) (Jonathan Scott).

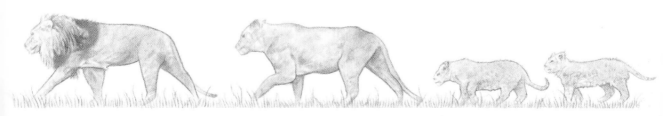

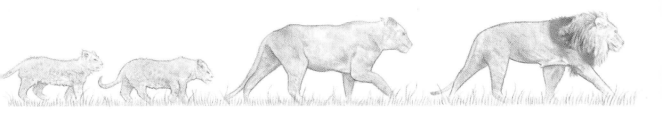

WHAT'S IT LIKE TO BE A
BABY LION?

by Honor Head

Illustrated by
Matthew Nicholas

The Millbrook Press
Brookfield, Connecticut

j599.757
HEA

Lions live in a large family group. They live in Africa and parts of India where it is very hot. Baby lions are called cubs. This book will tell you what it is like to be a lion cub.

13,15

W hen you read
this book imagine
that you are a
baby lion....

5

You are born in a safe hiding place away from the family. When you are born you are tiny. You cannot see and you cannot walk.

Y ou have one or two brothers or sisters born at the same time. You open your eyes a few days after you are born. Your eyes are a light gray-blue color at first. They will turn to a light brown color over the next few months.

Y ou learn to walk when
you are about three weeks
old. Until you can walk,
your mother carries you
from place to place in her
mouth.

She moves you from one hiding place to another at least once a week to keep you safe. After about six weeks your mother takes you to join the rest of the family group.

When you are a cub you have a fluffy, spotted coat. As you grow, the markings fade away. Your short tail will grow until it is quite long. It will have a little tuft of black hair at the end.

You have big, floppy paws with soft pads on the bottom and claws like needles. You use the rough bark of trees to sharpen your claws.

You live in a group called a pride. It will have about three adult males and six females. There will be other cubs of all ages. The lionesses hunt for food together, while the males stay behind to protect you and the other cubs from enemies.

You are very playful. You love to play fighting and hunting games. You chase the other cubs. You pretend you are hunting for food.

14

You play with a long twig and pretend it is food you have caught. Usually all the lionesses have their babies at the same time. This means you have lots of other cubs to play with.

You purr when you are happy and make little squealing noises. When you get older you will be able to roar loudly and growl.

16

When your mother wants you to follow her, she grunts softly. When she snarls at you and shows her teeth, it means she wants some peace and quiet.

You sleep for most of the day. You sleep on the ground or sometimes in the trees so that you do not get bitten by insects on the ground. The lionesses hunt in the early morning and in the evening when it is not so hot. After a big meal, you all have an extra-long sleep.

When you wake
up you have a
good, long stretch
and a big yawn.

You have a rough tongue covered with little spikes. When you lick your coat these spikes work like a brush and help to keep it clean. Your mother helps you keep your face clean.

Y ou can clean all parts of your body except the top of your head. You rub heads together to say hello and to be friendly.

You live on your mother's milk for the first few months of your life. You eat meat for the first time when you are about five months old.

Your mother and the other lionesses hunt for food. When they have killed an animal the male lions eat first, then the lionesses eat. Finally, you eat with the other cubs. You do not chew your food. You tear off pieces of meat and swallow them whole.

You drink once a day, early in the morning or after eating at night. You can go for many days without a drink. Sometimes you also go for many days without eating. When you are old enough your mother teaches you to hunt.

You learn to creep up on your prey through the long grass. You have to keep very quiet and still. You pretend your mother's tail is an animal. You watch it waving and then pounce on it.

W hen you are a year old you join your mother in the hunt for food. You follow her tail as a guide. Your coat is a sandy color, which helps to hide you in the long grass.

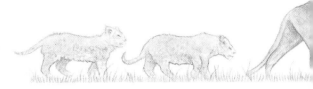

When you grow up you will have long, curved teeth and strong claws to help you catch your food.

If you are a male the hair on your head and neck will grow much longer and bushier. By the time you are three years old you will have a beautiful mane of hair.

Now you are as big as your mother. Soon you will leave the pride to find your own family. You are called the king of the beasts.

If you are a female you
will have your first babies
when you are three or four
years old. You carry the
babies inside you for
about three months.

When they are ready to be born, you will leave the pride and look for somewhere safe for your cubs to be born. You will look for a cave or the root of a tree. Both male and female lions live for about 20 years.

INDEX OF USEFUL WORDS

A baby lion
is called a cub.

A male lion
has a mane.

mane

coat

pads

paws

tail

A female lion is
called a lioness.